Fish Watching

with Eugenie Clark

by Michael Elsohn Ross

illustrations by
Wendy Smith

To Liam
Happy fish!
Watching
Michael Ross
2011

Carolrhoda Books, Inc./Minneapolis

To my dad, who taught me a true love of water and the life in it—M.E.R.

To the memory of Clif Coney—W.S.

The author and publisher gratefully acknowledge the assistance of Eugenie Clark and Bev Rodgerson of the University of Maryland Department of Biology.

Text copyright © 2000 by Michael Elsohn Ross
Illustrations copyright © 2000 by Wendy Smith

Carolrhoda Books, Inc.
A Division of Lerner Publishing Group
241 First Avenue North
Minneapolis, MN 55401 U.S.A.

Website address: www.lernerbooks.com

LIBRARY OF CONGRESS CATALOGING-IN-PUBLICATION DATA

Ross, Michael Elsohn, 1952–
  Fish watching with Eugenie Clark / by Michael Elsohn Ross ;
illustrations by Wendy Smith.
    p. cm. — (Naturalist's apprentice)
  Includes bibliographical references and index.
  Summary: Describes the life and career of ichthyologist Eugenie Clark, who began her research observing freshwater aquarium fishes and moved on to the underwater study of sharks and other marine animals. Includes observation tips and related activities.
    ISBN 1-57505-384-5
    1. Clark, Eugenie—Juvenile literature. 2. Ichthyologists—United States—Juvenile literature. 3. Women ichthyologists—United States—Juvenile literature. 4. Sharks—Research—Juvenile literature. 5. Fishes—Research—Juvenile literature. [1. Clark, Eugenie. 2. Ichthyologists. 3. Zoologists. 4. Sharks. 5. Fishes. 6. Women—Biography.] I. Smith, Wendy, ill. II. Title. III. Series: Ross, Michael Elsohn, 1952– Naturalist's apprentice.
QH31.C54R67 2000
597'.092—dc21
[B]
                                                                    99-19963

Manufactured in the United States of America
1 2 3 4 5 6 – JR – 05 04 03 02 01 00

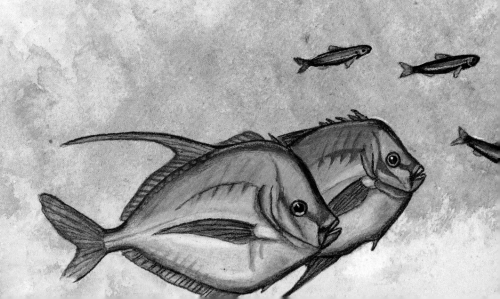

Contents

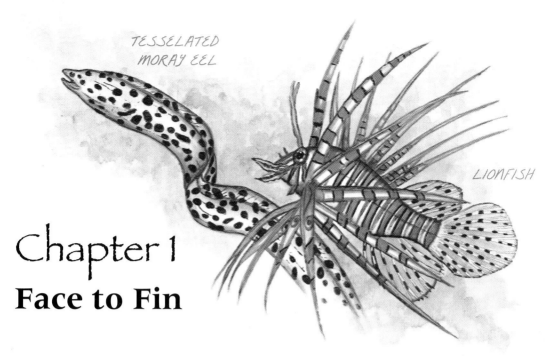

TESSELATED
MORAY EEL

LIONFISH

Chapter 1
Face to Fin

Have you ever watched a fish tank as if it were a never-ending movie? Maybe you've wondered what kinds of fish live in your local pond, river, or ocean. Can you see yourself exploring underwater worlds in search of creatures of the deep? Imagine spending your life as an **ichthyologist,** a scientist who investigates the mysterious lives of fish.

In 1931, a nine-year-old girl named Eugenie Clark dreamed about underwater adventures as she gazed intently into the aquarium at Battery Park in New York City. Genie pictured herself in the water, surrounded by beautifully colored fish. She pretended that she wore a large diving helmet and could walk on the ocean floor like the underwater **naturalists,** or students of nature, that she had read about. Little did Genie know that one day she would become a famous ichthyologist who would still be making new discoveries when she was more than seventy years old.

Genie was born in New York City in 1922. Her parents, Charles and Yumiko Clark, had always loved the water. Charles owned a private pool where Yumiko worked as a swimming instructor. Both were expert swimmers. Charles could even do trick dives, like diving from a high platform into a tiny pool. But one morning when Genie was a baby, something terrible happened. Her father went off for a swim in the ocean and was never seen again.

Baby Genie in Yumiko Clark's lap

Had Charles drowned, or been attacked by a shark? The family never found out what happened to him. Yumiko had to go to work full-time to support herself and baby Genie. Although Yumiko's job was in New York City, they moved to Atlantic City, New Jersey, to live with Genie's grandmother, Yuriko, and uncle, Boya. While Yumiko worked in New York during the week, Genie was taken care of by her grandmother.

Yumiko didn't let Charles's death end her family's love of swimming. She took her daughter to the beach soon after the little girl had started to walk. Even in the salty waves of the Atlantic Ocean, Genie liked to keep her eyes open so she could see what was on the bottom. She also loved to watch her mother, who could swim long distances gracefully. Genie didn't feel graceful in the water. Her strokes were clumsy and irregular. She felt like a pro only when she sat beside her mother on the beach, molding chewing gum into earplugs to keep the water out.

In 1928, the family moved to Queens, New York. Genie was ahead of her new classmates, so she skipped two grades during her first years at her new school. She also stood out because she was the school's only Japanese American student. (Genie's mother and grandmother had moved to the United States from Japan before Genie was born.) Although the family lived in the United States, they still followed many Japanese traditions. They ate their food

6

with chopsticks, and the food itself was different from what everyone else in the neighborhood ate. Breakfast was rice and seaweed. Dinner might be raw fish, octopus, sea urchin eggs, or cakes made from shark meat. When Genie told her classmates about the family's customs, they were amused and sometimes shocked. Still, she made many friends, such as Norma and Odette, whom she would know her whole life.

Genie's mother worked at a cigar and newspaper stand on the southern tip of Manhattan Island. From the stand, Genie could look out over the water and see the Statue of Liberty and the New Jersey shore. On Saturday mornings, she would sit behind the counter until her mother was free. Genie would get bored, but afterward came a real treat. Yumiko would take Genie to lunch at Fuji, a Japanese restaurant owned by their friend Masatomo Nobu, whom they called Nobusan. After lunch, Genie and her mother would share some special time together. They might see a movie, go shopping, or visit the zoo.

What's a Fish?

Fish live underwater, but so do many other creatures. What makes a fish a fish? If you've ever eaten one, you probably noticed its bones. All fish are **vertebrates,** animals that have backbones. To an ichthyologist, spineless aquatic **invertebrates** such as jellyfish and starfish aren't really fish. Fish have gills that enable them to breathe underwater. Most fish have a distinct head, a tail, and a variety of fins on their bodies. Like reptiles, fish are cold-blooded—they can't control their body temperature the way that mammals can.

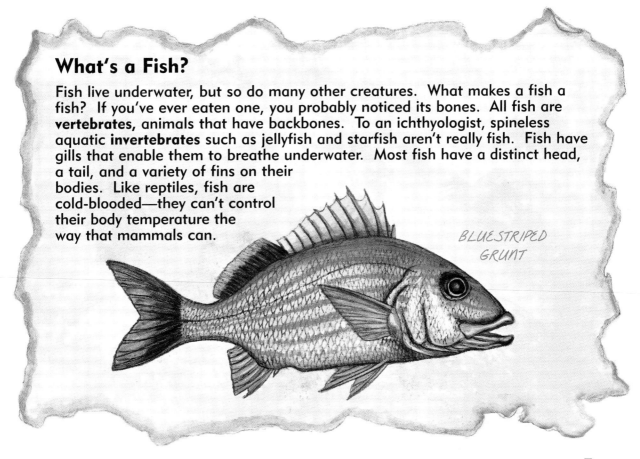

BLUESTRIPED GRUNT

It was on one of these afternoons that Genie and her mother first visited the aquarium at Battery Park. After that, Genie wanted to go there every Saturday afternoon. Yumiko enjoyed the aquarium, but Genie could never get her to stay long enough. Finally, one Saturday morning Genie convinced her mother to drop her off at the aquarium instead of making her sit behind the counter at the cigar stand. Genie was thrilled. Throughout the large building were tanks of underwater creatures, but she was drawn to the large tank at the back, where the water seemed to go on forever. Face pressed close to the glass, Genie would daydream that she was deep underwater, surrounded by swimming sharks and other fish.

Saturday after Saturday, Genie returned to the aquarium. She had been hooked by the Battery Park fish! Soon she made a group of new friends—the homeless men who slept in the park. When the men came into the aquarium to get out of the rain, Genie shared with them what she had learned about different fish.

Genie had always enjoyed watching her mother and other expert swimmers. As she stared at the best swimmers of all—fish—she wondered how they moved so effortlessly. How did they get along without arms and legs for stroking through the water? Eventually, Genie realized that fish don't swim like people. They use their fins and tails primarily for changing direction and keeping their balance. It's their strong, wriggling muscles that push them through the water.

When December came, Genie told her mother that she wanted nothing for Christmas but a fish tank of her own. There wasn't much money for presents, though. The United States was going

Window Watching

An aquarium is like a window into the underwater world. Visit one. It doesn't matter if you don't live near a large city aquarium like the one Genie visited in New York. A small aquarium will do just fine. You may have a friend or relative who keeps fish. Or visit a pet store and gaze at the fish on display.

Like Genie, you may wonder how fish swim or what they eat. You might even want to learn the names of the fish you see. Honor your curiosity by writing down your questions. The more fish you watch, the more likely you'll discover your answers floating by.

through a severe economic depression, and many people didn't have jobs. People who did have work usually had little money to spare. Even Genie's allowance of ten cents a week had been set aside for the family's expenses.

Still, Genie tried to bargain for fish. She had to trade away future Christmas and birthday presents, but before long Yumiko purchased a large tank, aquatic plants, snails, and fish. Genie could watch fish at home! Among her first fish were pairs of guppies, black speckled platys, and pale green swordtails, plus a colorful clown fish.

As Genie grew older, her interest in collecting and studying fish increased. She read many books and articles about fish. Among her favorites were those by William Beebe, a famous naturalist who was amazing the world with his deep-sea dives in an underwater vehicle called a bathysphere. Genie loved his descriptions of the strange, fascinating fish of the ocean deep.

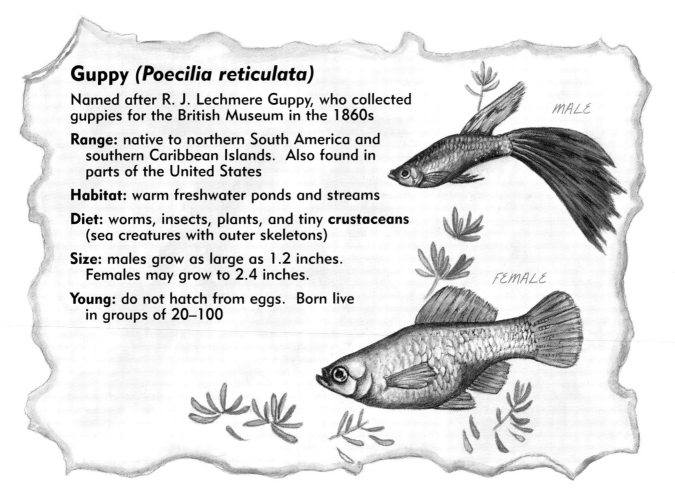

Guppy (*Poecilia reticulata*)

Named after R. J. Lechmere Guppy, who collected guppies for the British Museum in the 1860s

Range: native to northern South America and southern Caribbean Islands. Also found in parts of the United States

Habitat: warm freshwater ponds and streams

Diet: worms, insects, plants, and tiny **crustaceans** (sea creatures with outer skeletons)

Size: males grow as large as 1.2 inches. Females may grow to 2.4 inches.

Young: do not hatch from eggs. Born live in groups of 20–100

MALE

FEMALE

Ready for Fish?

Are you interested in hosting a few fish of your own? Here are some things to think about before you get started:

✔ Owning any type of pet is a big responsibility. Your fish will depend on you to provide proper food; the right amount of light; gravel; and clean, filtered, properly heated water. To learn more about the needs of fish, visit your local library or bookstore and read about keeping fish as pets.

✔ Starting a fish tank can be expensive. A twenty-gallon tank, equipment, and fish may cost over a hundred dollars. Consider asking a teacher if you could start a classroom tank.

✔ If you and your parents decide you're ready to host fish, talk to a fish expert at a pet store. Many stores offer basic aquarium kits with all the equipment you'll need. Guppies, platys, and tetras are suitable for a basic aquarium.

✔ For a simpler and even less expensive aquarium, consider a ten-gallon tank with bettas or goldfish. They require less space and equipment than many other types of fish.

Genie kept notes on her fish and excitedly watched them grow, mate, and give birth. One day, she and her mother witnessed an amazing event—the mating of Genie's bettas. The male constructed a nest of air bubbles, then squeezed the female with his long fins until her eggs came out. With great care, the male picked up each egg in his mouth and dropped it on the bubble nest.

When would the eggs hatch? Genie and Yumiko watched carefully. A few days later, they noticed tiny baby fish hanging from the nest. Before long, the tank was swarming with over a hundred of them. Genie had visions of making a fortune raising and selling bettas, until she realized that raising young fish wasn't as easy as it seemed. Many of the babies were eaten by bigger fish, and only a few survived to adulthood.

Although Genie didn't become a fish rancher, her passion for aquatic creatures kept growing. In high school, her favorite course was **biology,** the study of living things. The more she learned about animal biology, the more she understood about the behavior of her aquarium fish—and the more fishy questions she had.

MALE BETTA
CONSTRUCTING
NEST

Chapter 2
Fish School

When Genie finished high school in 1938, she was only sixteen years old. She was accepted into Hunter College, a women's college in New York City. Hunter was free to New York residents with high grades. There was no doubt in Genie's mind that she would major in **zoology,** the study of animals. She hoped to become an ichthyologist and an explorer like William Beebe.

In the 1930s, most scientists in the United States were men. Many women didn't go to college, and those who did often entered teaching or other traditionally female fields. Genie's family suggested that she take typing and shorthand along with her zoology courses. "In case you don't find a job like Dr. Beebe's when you finish college," they said, "you might get a start as some famous ichthyologist's secretary." But Genie had her fish to care for and lots of zoology classes to attend. She had no time for extra courses. Besides, she wasn't interested in being a secretary. She aimed to be a famous ichthyologist herself!

Although Genie studied hard, she had trouble keeping her grades up because she kept falling asleep in class. After her first semester, she was suspended from school. Then she went to a doctor who realized that she was suffering from anemia, a lack of red blood cells. Rest and a special diet helped Genie to recover and return to school.

Changes were happening not only in Genie's life, but all over the world. In 1939, World War II began, as Japan, Germany, and Italy fought to take over countries in Asia, Africa, and Europe. The United States didn't enter the war immediately, but many people thought the Americans would join the fighting soon.

For the time being, though, Genie focused on her work. She took as many zoology classes as she could. For her course in **anatomy**—the study of the structure of living things—Genie spent hours in Hunter's laboratories. There, she dissected, or cut open, dead animals to learn about their body structure.

Genie (right) and Norma in 1940

Looking at dead animals was fine with Genie, but learning about live ones was even more fascinating. During her summer break, Genie took field classes at the University of Michigan's Biological Station. There, she and her old friend Norma, who was also a zoology student, collected fish and snakes. It wasn't easy to wake up at 3:45 A.M. to watch birds for their ornithology (bird study) class. But before long they looked forward to hearing the tunes of songbirds.

While celebrating at her mother's birthday party on December 7, 1941, Genie heard the terrible news that Japan had dropped bombs on the United States naval base at Pearl Harbor, Hawaii. The entire family was shocked. Within weeks, Japanese Americans on the West Coast were rounded up and sent to internment camps. (The army claimed that these people may have posed danger to the United States.) Would the same thing happen to Genie's family? The Clarks' friend Nobusan was harassed at his restaurant by angry Americans who blamed the bombing on all Japanese people—even those who didn't live in Japan. Soon Nobusan changed the name of his restaurant to make it sound less Japanese.

Swimsuit Survey

You may not have the chance to dissect fish in a laboratory like Genie did, but you can still learn a lot about fish anatomy with your eyes. You'll see that just as there are many styles of swimsuits for people, so are there variations in the swimsuits that fish "wear." Be sure to write down your observations and questions.

Supplies
✔ pen or pencil
✔ notebook

What to Do

✔ Look at the diagram below, then carefully watch a cruising fish. Can you locate all the parts that are labeled on the diagram? Watch carefully to see if you can tell what each type of fin is used for.

✔ Check out another type of fish and compare it to the first one. Do both fish have the same number of fins? Are their fins and bodies shaped the same? See if you can tell what type of body structure the best swimmer has.

✔ Look at the mouths of the fish you're observing. Are they shaped the same way? How do the fish use their mouths to get food?

✔ Next, look at the eyes. Are they in the same spot on both fish? Are they shaped the same?

✔ Examine the skin colors and patterns. How do they differ on the two types of fish? Can you think of any reasons why fish might be colored differently?

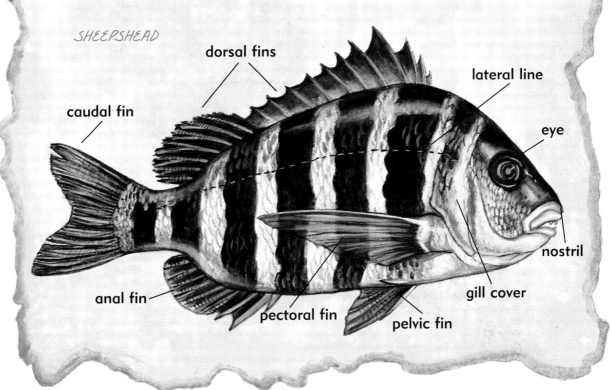

SHEEPSHEAD

dorsal fins

lateral line

caudal fin

eye

nostril

anal fin

gill cover

pectoral fin

pelvic fin

Fortunately, the Japanese Americans on the East Coast were not put into camps. Genie was able to keep going to school, and in 1942 she graduated from Hunter with a degree in zoology and high hopes to continue her education. But when she applied to a graduate program at Columbia University, a professor told her, "I can tell by looking at you, if you do finish [graduate school] you will probably get married, have a bunch of kids, and never do anything in science after we have invested our time and money in you."

The Columbia professor was right about one thing. That very year, Genie married a pilot named Hideo "Roy" Umaki. Soon after their wedding, Roy was drafted into the army and sent overseas. It was up to Genie to support herself. True to her family's prediction, there were no jobs waiting for young ichthyologists. But there were jobs for chemists. Genie and Norma had both studied chemistry in college, and they found jobs at a plastics research center across the Hudson River in Newark, New Jersey.

Of course, the Columbia professor was wrong when he imagined that Genie would give up her passion for studying fish. She and Norma quickly signed up for evening graduate courses at New York University. It was hard to stay awake for some classes after working all day, but Genie had no problem with her ichthyology class. Her

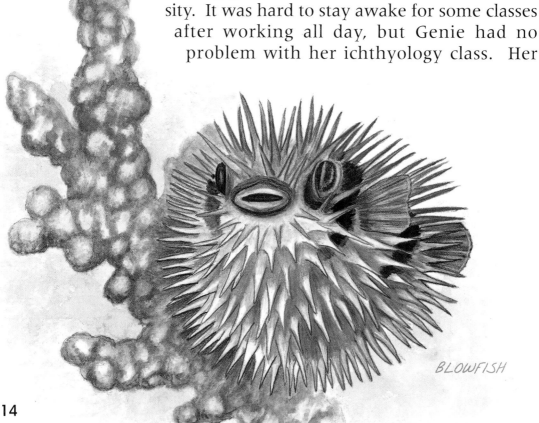

BLOWFISH

professor was none other than Dr. Charles M. Breder Jr., the former head of the aquarium at Battery Park. Dr. Breder was in charge of the fish collections at the American Museum of Natural History, where the class was taught. Genie was learning from a world-famous fish expert.

Dr. Breder encouraged Genie to study the blowfish, a strange fish that puffs up and pokes out its spines like an underwater porcupine. How did blowfish puff up? Patiently Genie experimented with pumping up the stomachs of dead blowfish. She wrote careful notes and sketched detailed drawings. Her research paid off. After Genie completed her study, Dr. Breder asked if he could combine her results with his work and publish a joint paper on their findings. The girl who had stared at aquarium fish at Battery Park was teamed up in print with one of the world's finest ichthyologists!

Quick Draw

From her earliest years as an aquarium owner, Genie made sketches of fish to record her experiments and to illustrate her reports. Like Genie, you may find that sketching helps you to discover new details and new questions about the fish you're drawing. Let your pen or pencil lead the way!

Supplies
✔ sketchbook or scrap paper
✔ clipboard or other hard writing surface
✔ pen or pencil
✔ colored pencils or markers

What to Do
✔ Start by watching a fish closely for several minutes. Look at the outline of its body and sketch it. What other lines make up the fish's shape? What shapes are its fins? Does it have spines? Add these lines to your sketch.

✔ Before you make a detailed drawing of the entire fish, try focusing on its individual parts.

Make some quick sketches of the fish's fins, mouth, and eyes.

✔ See if you can match some of the colors or patterns that you notice on the fish's skin.

✔ When you feel ready to bring all these details together, try creating a picture of the whole fish.

Nobusan, Yumiko, Grandmother Yuriko, and Uncle Boya in the late 1940s

Soon another famous fish expert crossed Genie's path. In the summer of 1946, Dr. Carl L. Hubbs offered Genie a job as a part-time research assistant at the Scripps Institution of Oceanography in La Jolla, California. Genie would be able to complete further fish studies and work on a Ph.D. in ichthyology. Soon after she went, her mother married Nobusan, their friend who ran the Japanese restaurant. He had been like part of the family for a long time, and Genie was delighted to have him as a stepfather.

Genie began her new studies at the end of the summer. Day after day, she counted the rays, tiny rods that support the fins, of sculpins. She also counted their vertebrae, or segments of the backbone. Her counts revealed that populations of the same **species,** or kind, of sculpin weren't always the same. When they came from different areas, the sculpin populations sometimes had different numbers of rays and vertebrae. Genie realized that this was an example of how animals evolve, or change very slowly over time. When populations of the same type of fish lived in different places, they could gradually evolve until they were no longer exactly the same.

Besides doing lab work, Genie attended classes. Best of all, she went on frequent trips out to sea on the institution's ship. She learned how to collect fish from the sea bottom, take water samples, and measure the water temperature at different depths.

One day, Dr. Hubbs caught a swell shark and brought it back alive to the lab. The swell shark is the only type of shark that can puff itself up. How did it do this? Dr. Hubbs asked Genie to investigate. As she had done with the blowfish, Genie carefully examined the swell shark's anatomy. Soon she discovered that its stomach could expand like a balloon. But she was still baffled as to why it would do so. Other fish make themselves bigger to avoid being eaten, but what would want to eat a shark? Genie learned that scientific discovery can lead to questions as well as answers.

SWELL SHARK

Along the rocky reefs near the institution, Genie had her first experience swimming with a face mask. Instead of looking through the glass of an aquarium wall, she wore a glass plate in front of her eyes. Genie liked being able to see well underwater, but she wanted to dive deeper and stay underwater longer. Dr. Hubbs promised her a chance to make a helmet dive. In the 1940s, modern scuba gear was not yet commonly used. Divers who wanted to spend long periods of time underwater wore a heavy metal helmet. A line connected the helmet to an air pump in the boat above, allowing the diver to breathe.

The Well-Equipped Fish Watcher

If you have the opportunity to snorkel in a pond, lake, or ocean, you may be able to catch close-up views of wild fish. Be sure to swim only when accompanied by an adult.

snorkel

mask

swimsuit

flippers

When the day for Genie's first helmet dive finally came, she was tense with excitement. She would be the only woman in a group of five divers. After a couple of the men had gone down, it was Genie's turn. Down, down, down she dropped. The bottom was twenty-eight feet below the surface. Underwater plants waved back and forth in the currents like tall grass in a wind. Above, Genie could see the underside of the ship. Around her swam all sorts of fish. One even peeked into her helmet's face plate.

The dive was thrilling, but it got too exciting when Genie was knocked over by underwater currents and stopped getting air through her line. She turned the air valve, but she couldn't get any more air. Just as she was about to pass out, Genie pulled off the heavy helmet and floated to the surface, where she was rescued.

Wrapped in blankets, holding a cup of hot coffee, Genie told the other divers about how her air supply was cut off. "Just like a woman to screw the valve the wrong way and cut off her air," one of the men remarked. But when the divers checked the equipment, they found that the air hose had been leaking. The incident wasn't Genie's fault, and it wasn't her last dive. Later that day, she dove again, and her many helmet dives after that were accident free.

Very few women had explored and studied as Genie was doing. With the help of Dr. Hubbs and her other mentors, she had become a pioneer. Yet even under the sponsorship of colleagues who respected her, she didn't gain the same experience that the male students did. For example, she wasn't allowed to go on overnight trips on the research ship because it wasn't considered proper for a woman to sleep in the same quarters as men. Although restrictions like this one were frustrating, Genie was grateful for the encouragement of Dr. Hubbs and other scientists. She focused on her work with more determination than ever.

BLUE-SPOTTED STINGRAY

19

In 1947, when Genie was twenty-five, she was hired by the U.S. Fish and Wildlife Service to study fish in the Philippine Islands. She would be the only female scientist in the entire organization. On her way to the Philippines, Genie stopped in Hawaii, where she was able to see her husband for the first time in several long years. They had been away from each other more than they had been together. Not long after this visit, Genie and Roy decided to divorce.

While Genie was in Hawaii, she was told that her trip would be delayed because the FBI had to check out her Japanese background. But the war with Japan was over. Was the government having doubts about hiring a woman? It was easy for Genie to keep busy swimming and studying fish, but she soon got the feeling that she wasn't going to be cleared for the job. After two weeks, she discovered that a man had been hired in her place, and the group had taken off without her! She had already been in touch with Dr. Albert Herre, an expert on Philippine fish, and was upset that she wouldn't have a chance to work with him. Fortunately, she had enjoyed studying puffer fish while she waited.

Later Genie realized that the FBI had done her a favor. If she had gone to the Philippines, she wouldn't have returned to New York. There, Dr. Myron Gordon offered her the chance to continue working on her Ph.D. He wanted her to study at New York University and become his research assistant at the American Museum of Natural History. Genie's job would be to study the mating behaviors of platys and swordtails—some of the first fish she had kept in her home aquarium! Genie happily accepted this wonderful offer.

EGG CASE OF LESSER SPOTTED DOGFISH

KELP

Southern Platy *(Xiphophorus maculatus)*

Range: native to freshwater ponds and streams in southern Mexico and Central America. Also found in Florida and other parts of the United States

Habitat: freshwater ponds and streams

Diet: worms, crustaceans, insects, plants

Size: males may grow as large as 1.6 inches. Females may grow to 2.4 inches.

Young: born live in groups of 10–80

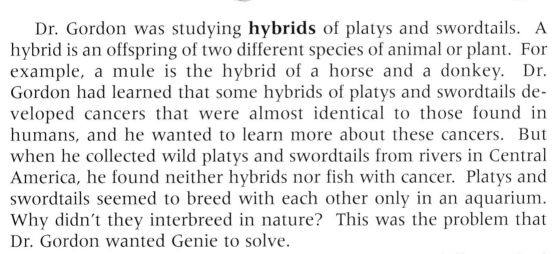

Dr. Gordon was studying **hybrids** of platys and swordtails. A hybrid is an offspring of two different species of animal or plant. For example, a mule is the hybrid of a horse and a donkey. Dr. Gordon had learned that some hybrids of platys and swordtails developed cancers that were almost identical to those found in humans, and he wanted to learn more about these cancers. But when he collected wild platys and swordtails from rivers in Central America, he found neither hybrids nor fish with cancer. Platys and swordtails seemed to breed with each other only in an aquarium. Why didn't they interbreed in nature? This was the problem that Dr. Gordon wanted Genie to solve.

In the hot, humid museum greenhouse, Genie carefully watched the platys and swordtails. Her first job was to figure out exactly when and how the fish mated. When animals mate, the male provides sperm cells that fertilize the female's eggs, making the eggs able to grow. Most fish mate externally, meaning that the female lays eggs and the male releases sperm that mix with them. Genie already knew that male platys and swordtails inserted sperm into the female's body. The eggs are fertilized and grow within the female, which gives birth to live young. But how could Genie tell when mating occurred?

Green Swordtail (*Xiphophorus helleri*)

Only male swordtails have the swordlike tail that gives this fish its name.

Range: native to southern Mexico and Central America. Also found in Florida and other parts of the United States

Habitat: freshwater ponds and streams

Diet: worms, crustaceans, insects, plants

Size: males may grow as large as 4 inches. Females may grow to 4.7 inches.

Young: born live in groups of 20–100

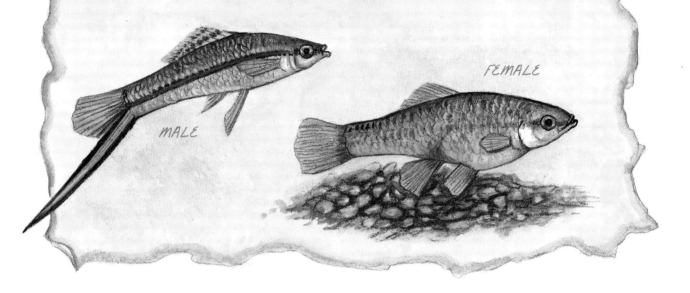

MALE

FEMALE

Most people who studied platys and swordtails thought that mating occurred when a male touched a female with his anal fin. This behavior might happen as often as a hundred times in ten minutes. Genie wondered if the fish really mated that frequently, especially after she witnessed a much less common behavior. After the fish had been apart for a while, they joined together for several seconds, almost as though they were glued.

Genie thought that this "gluing" was the actual mating, and she decided to try to prove it. She placed female fish in a tank with a male for ten minutes and watched how the fish behaved. Then she carefully examined the female, using a microscope to look for sperm from the male. After examining many female fish, Genie was certain that only those that joined together had truly mated.

Once Genie had learned how platys and swordtails mated, she could explore why they didn't produce hybrid young in the wild. She set up a long series of experiments. Eventually, she learned that a female preferred to mate with a male of her own species. In the wild, she could always find such a male. After mating, she stored the sperm inside her body for up to a year. The stored sperm enabled the females to produce young every four or five weeks. The female might mate with a male of a different species during this time, but only the sperm that she had already stored would fertilize her eggs. That was one reason why Dr. Gordon hadn't found any hybrids in the wild. But if a female without any stored sperm was kept in an aquarium with a male of another species, the fish would mate and hybrids would result.

Ichthyological Spying

You've done some fishy anatomical studies, but what can you learn about the behaviors of fish? Like Eugenie Clark, you can take a close look at the fish around you and try to understand what they do and why.

Supplies
✔ notebook
✔ pen or pencil

What to Do
✔ Start by spying on fish in a tank, pond, or stream. Write down any questions you have about their behavior, then make notes on the clues you spot.

✔ Try to keep track of a single fish for several minutes or longer. How does it spend its time?

✔ How do the fish interact with each other? Do they move in schools, or groups of fish? Or are they loners?

✔ How do the fish find and eat food? If you're watching aquarium fish, note how they behave when you feed them. Are some fish better at reaching the food than others?

✔ Where do the fish hang out? Do they prefer light or dark places? Do they hide or swim out in the open?

✔ Can you find differences in the behaviors of individuals of the same species?

Chapter 3
Underwater Adventures

Genie spent three intense years studying swordtails and platys, but she did take some breaks from fish-tank observations in New York. She traveled to Bimini in the West Indies to catch and study filefish. These unusual fish could change colors and even stand on their head.

Genie also tested the vision and memory of gobies. Gobies are small fish that often live in tide pools, shallow pools of ocean water that remain on the shore after the tide goes out. Unlike people, most fish (including gobies) have eyes on either side of the head. Genie and a biologist named Dr. Roger Sperry wanted to find out whether this eye placement affects how fish learn. Dr. Sperry had been studying how the two halves of the brain, the right and left, work together. Could information be transferred from an eye on one side of the head to the opposite side of the brain?

Like little pirates, the gobies were fitted with eye patches and taught to find food on a line lowered into the tanks. After the gobies had mastered the lesson, Genie and Dr. Sperry moved the patches to the other eye. Some of the gobies knew exactly where to find the food. But some seemed puzzled, and others were completely confused and had to start learning all over again. At first, Genie was frustrated by the mixed results, but Dr. Sperry reminded her that individuals, whether they are fish or people, could vary in their ability to learn.

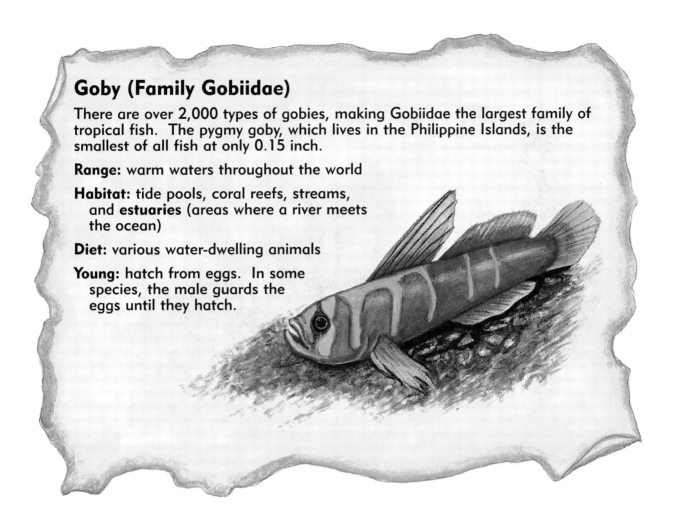

Goby (Family Gobiidae)

There are over 2,000 types of gobies, making Gobiidae the largest family of tropical fish. The pygmy goby, which lives in the Philippine Islands, is the smallest of all fish at only 0.15 inch.

Range: warm waters throughout the world

Habitat: tide pools, coral reefs, streams, and **estuaries** (areas where a river meets the ocean)

Diet: various water-dwelling animals

Young: hatch from eggs. In some species, the male guards the eggs until they hatch.

In 1949, as Genie neared the end of her platy and swordtail studies, she learned about a new opportunity. The Pacific Science Board was looking for biologists to conduct studies in Micronesia, a group of islands east of the Philippines. Genie proposed a study of the region's fish, especially the poisonous ones. She also wanted to collect fish for the American Museum of Natural History. The board awarded her a research fellowship, and in June she was on her way.

Soon Genie was traveling from one beautiful tropical island to another, talking with fishers and collecting specimens. Because the fish she collected were for a museum, they had to be killed. Genie visited shallow tide pools and used a special poison, rotenone, to knock out the fish. Then she preserved them in a chemical called formalin. Later she transferred them to alcohol for shipping. These fish had to be handled with care—some, like the scorpion fish, had poisonous spines on their fins.

SQUID

On the island of Guam, Genie went out to sea with one of the best fishers on the island. For lunch, he offered her a freshly caught raw squid. No doubt it was a test. Would the woman scientist swallow the slimy meal? Genie had eaten raw squid at her stepfather's restaurant, but it had been thinly sliced and artistically prepared. Here, she was expected to bite a chunk out of a whole squid. With little hesitation, she took a bite and found that it wasn't bad. Genie's trust sealed her friendship with the fisher, and she was treated as an honored guest.

In the island nation of Palau, Genie met a skilled spearfisher named Siakong. Wearing homemade goggles, Siakong would dive deep below the surface and lurk on a reef, lying in wait for passing fish. The moment a fish came near, his lightweight bamboo spear darted forward, capturing another specimen for science. Siakong also threw a net to catch fish from the boat. Thanks to his efforts, Genie was able to collect many unusual species of fish. As she learned to use the spear and net herself, she developed an even greater appreciation of Siakong's skill.

Genie felt like she was in paradise. She encountered many sea creatures that she had never seen in the wild, such as triggerfish, puffers, and giant clams. There was plenty of work to do, preserving and cataloging specimens after each collecting trip, but Genie was full of energy. She loved being surrounded by the awesome beauty of the reefs, the coconut-fringed islands, and the endless sky. The customs of the people she met intrigued her, too. On an island called Mogmog, she was introduced to the king. Genie had never dreamed that she would meet a monarch while wearing a bathing suit—or that the monarch would be dressed in a loincloth and covered with tattoos.

Fish Catch

On your next trip to a pond, a lake, a stream, or the seashore, try to catch small fish such as minnows for a quick examination. Catching fish takes lots of practice, so don't get discouraged if it takes a while. Unlike Genie, you aren't collecting dead fish for a museum, so be sure to handle your catch with care and return the fish to the water when you're done.

Warning: Try this activity only when an adult is nearby, and stay in shallow water. Before you start, check with your state's fish and game department to see if it is legal to catch, examine, and release small fish where you live. (The number should be listed in the government section of the phone book.)

Supplies
✔ plastic container
✔ small fishnet
✔ towel

What to Do
✔ Fill the plastic container with water from the area where you're fishing. Keep the container nearby, ready to receive your catch.

✔ Stand quietly in shallow water, holding the fishnet just over the surface.

✔ When a fish swims by, try to scoop it up. Quickly transfer the netted fish into your container for observation.

✔ You can also use a towel to scoop up small fish from a shallow pool. With a friend's help, place the towel on the bottom of the pool. Stand at opposite ends, holding a corner of the towel in each hand. As a fish swims over the towel, pull it up quickly. Be ready to dump your catch into the plastic container.

A fishing trip on the Red Sea

When her trip ended, Genie returned to New York with wonderful memories. But her travels didn't end there. In 1950, she was awarded a Ph.D. for her studies of platys, swordtails, and guppies. Soon after, she received a Fulbright scholarship to go to Egypt, to study the fish of the Red Sea. But Genie wasn't sure what a year in Egypt would do for her love life. She had recently met a handsome young doctor from Greece, Ilias Papakonstantinou. Ilias gave Genie great support in her work, and she fell in love with him. But would their relationship last when they were thousands of miles apart? Before Genie left for Egypt, they quickly married at a courthouse in New York.

Genie found another kind of paradise at her new home, the Marine Biological Station, a few miles north of the town of Al Ghurdaqah. She lived in a comfortable cottage and had aquariums for keeping fish. Just a short swim from the station was a magnificent coral reef where she could observe fish in the wild, then collect them for further studies in the lab. She also went out with the area's fishers, who helped her capture pipefish and sea horses. Genie kept notes on all the fish she collected, dissected many specimens, and sketched the anatomy of rare fish. Most important of all, she found three new fish species! Sometimes she worked late into the night. After a long day, she would often dash off a letter to Ilias, describing her incredible experiences in the sea.

In June, Ilias came to visit, and he and Genie went to Cairo to have a religious wedding ceremony at a Greek Orthodox church. Afterward they spent day after glorious day diving in the Red Sea. Ilias loved to swim as much as Genie did, and he took quickly to the sport of spearfishing. Just as he was becoming an expert at catching fish for her, the vacation ended. Ilias returned to work in Buffalo, New York. When Genie finished her work in Egypt and joined Ilias in Buffalo, winter had begun. As Genie looked out the window at the snowy landscape, she wrote her reports and dreamed of tropical waters.

Chapter 4
Scuba Mom

In 1952, Eugenie Clark was twenty-nine years old, married, and expecting her first child. Would she give up on science, as the Columbia University professor had predicted years before? Of course not! As her child grew within her, Genie set to work writing about her studies and experiences. A year before, she had published an article in *Natural History* magazine about her adventures in the South Seas. Then a book editor asked Genie to write the entire story of her career. *Lady with a Spear* was published in 1953. Readers were captivated by the story of the woman scientist whose childhood dream had come alive, and the book became a huge success.

Genie's daughter Hera was born at the end of 1952, and soon the family moved to New York City. Genie went to work as a biology instructor at Hunter College, where she had once gone to school. Then she received an invitation from Anne and William H. Vanderbilt to visit their estate in Englewood, Florida. There, Genie learned that the Vanderbilts wanted to start a marine laboratory—and they wanted her to be the lab's director!

By this time, Genie was pregnant again. She and Ilias decided that Florida would be a great place to raise their kids. Ilias arranged to open a medical practice in Venice, not far from the lab's location in Placida. Soon after their second daughter, Aya, was born in 1954, the family moved to a sunny beach house.

Genie observes a specimen at the Cape Haze Marine Laboratory.

Genie found a babysitter to watch the girls while she worked on plans for the lab with Beryl Chadwick, an expert local fisher. Soon the Cape Haze Marine Laboratory had a small lab building, a dock, and one of the Vanderbilts' boats to use. Genie and her new colleagues tracked down some used lab equipment and began to collect and study the local marine life.

Scientists came from all over the country to study at the lab. When Dr. John Heller came to study shark livers for his medical research, Genie had her first experience catching sharks. Beryl anchored each end of a line with heavy weights, then baited the line with mullet fish. Two sharks took the bait and were towed back to the lab. Dissecting a five-hundred-pound shark was amazing, but Dr. Heller thought that live sharks would be more helpful for his research. So they set up more bait and built a pen in shallow water for their large guests.

Genie's life grew even busier with the needs of her work and her family. Her parents, Yumiko and Nobusan, moved their restaurant from New York to a small town near the lab. Genie was glad for both their company and the babysitting help that Yumiko offered. The family soon settled into their new life along the seashore. In May of 1956, Genie gave birth to a little boy with a big name—Themistokles Alexander Konstantinou. (Ilias had shortened his last name, but the baby's name was still so long that he was later nicknamed Tak.)

A few weeks later, Genie tried out the lab's new scuba gear to investigate an intriguing puzzle. The year before, she had found a number of fish called belted sand bass. She thought the fish were females because they were carrying eggs, but she was surprised to find no males nearby for them to mate with. But she'd had no time to investigate further.

When Genie went looking for the belted sand bass again, she found and collected several females. Then she discussed her questions with her former teacher Dr. Breder, who was visiting the lab. At his suggestion, Genie examined the fish's ovaries, the organs that produce eggs, under a microscope. She was amazed to discover that in addition to eggs, each bass also produced sperm. No wonder she hadn't found any male fish. The belted sand bass were **hermaphrodites** (hur-MAFF-ruh-dites), animals with both male and female parts!

After more study, Genie learned that a single belted sand bass can act as a male, providing sperm, and as a female, laying eggs. Each fish can switch roles from male to female several times in a single hour. The fish also change colors when they switch roles. They are the only fish known to do this. Acting as a male, a belted sand bass has dark stripes, or bands, while as a female it is unbanded. Genie found that after a few days in captivity, the belted sand bass no longer mated at all. This was why no one had ever witnessed their unusual mating behavior.

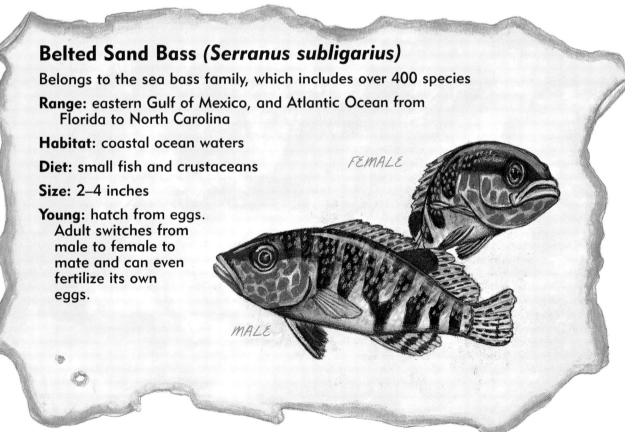

Belted Sand Bass (*Serranus subligarius*)

Belongs to the sea bass family, which includes over 400 species

Range: eastern Gulf of Mexico, and Atlantic Ocean from Florida to North Carolina

Habitat: coastal ocean waters

Diet: small fish and crustaceans

Size: 2–4 inches

Young: hatch from eggs. Adult switches from male to female to mate and can even fertilize its own eggs.

FEMALE

MALE

In the summer of 1958, another visitor, Dr. Lester Aronson, came to the lab. Genie was pregnant once again, and she said she felt more like a "Lady with a Sphere" than a "Lady with a Spear." But she was still comfortable diving, and she was ready for a new chapter in her work—one that Dr. Aronson, an expert in animal behavior, could help her begin.

Genie asked Dr. Aronson if anyone had ever studied the learning behavior of sharks. For years, scientists such as B. F. Skinner had studied how pigeons and rats learn. But most scientists thought that sharks were stupid and would therefore make poor learners. Genie and her helpers at the lab weren't so sure. They had noticed that when people approached the lab's shark tank, the captive lemon sharks always swam toward them, expecting to be fed. If the sharks could learn that people brought food, perhaps they could be taught other things.

Examining nurse sharks on the Cape Haze dock at night

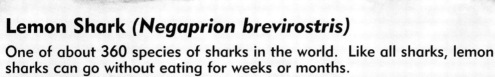

Lemon Shark (*Negaprion brevirostris*)

One of about 360 species of sharks in the world. Like all sharks, lemon sharks can go without eating for weeks or months.

Range: western Atlantic Ocean from New Jersey to Brazil, plus eastern Pacific Ocean

Habitat: close to shore and occasionally in river mouths

Diet: small fish, crustaceans

Size: up to about 12 feet

Young: born live

Dr. Aronson didn't know of anyone who had studied shark learning behaviors, and he was enthusiastic about setting up an experiment. He and Genie created a plan to teach a lemon shark to bump its nose against a target to get food. The target was simply a square of wood, painted white and attached to a wooden arm. It was placed underwater during the feeding tests and connected to a bell. When a shark gave the target a hefty push, the bell would ring, and the shark would be fed.

Soon Dr. Aronson had to return to New York, but Genie started the experiment with the help of her coworkers. Two lemon sharks, a female and a male, were used in the experiments. The first step was to get the sharks used to the target. Genie and her colleagues began by dangling fish from a string in front of the target until the sharks took the food. Each day, the food was moved closer and closer to the target. Eventually the sharks bumped into the target, causing the bell to ring.

To keep the sharks eager to take the fish, Genie put them on a diet. The sharks were served only small portions of fish during each test. Soon they had to ring the bell as many as ten times a day to get their food. As the tests were repeated, the sharks started to hit the target faster and faster.

After six weeks, Genie put the target in the water without dangling any fish in front of it. What would the sharks do? The male shark, L-2, swam past the target but didn't hit it. L-2 passed the target nine more times before he finally gave it a good nudge with his nose. When the bell rang, he was tossed some fish. It took three days for L-1, the female shark, to catch on, but soon both sharks were ringing the target to get food. Genie and her colleagues had proven that lemon sharks could be taught!

Genie noticed that the sharks always seemed to turn to the right after pushing the target, and she decided to see if she could change this habit. Eventually the scientists taught the sharks to push the target, turn to the left, and swim eight feet to catch fish dropped for them. Visitors to the lab were impressed. They had seen trained porpoises and seals, but had never thought a shark had the intelligence to learn these sorts of tricks.

Fish Experiments

You probably have some questions of your own about the fish you watch. Can you devise any experiments to help you answer your questions or to test your ideas? Here are a few suggestions to get you started. Remember to keep records of your tests!

✔ Try to teach a fish to come to a certain place each day to look for food, or to look for food when you ring a bell or thump on a hard object. Perhaps you can feed your fish at the same time each day to see if they will eventually look for a meal at that time.

✔ You may have noticed that the fish you watch like to hide in a special place. Try changing the location of objects in the water to give your fish new and different hiding places. How do they respond?

Genie, Ilias, and their four children in about 1960

In October of 1958, Genie and Ilias's second son, Nikolas, was born. Genie was the mother of four young children, and she kept on working with her shark classroom as well. That December, when the water grew cooler, the sharks lost interest in eating for about ten weeks. Genie wondered if the sharks would remember their lessons after such a long winter vacation. On February 19, she watched in amazement as L-1 and L-2 fed for the first time that year by pressing the target.

Genie ran more experiments with the lemon sharks and found that they could learn to recognize targets of different shapes and colors. She spent some time outside the lab, too. She gave lectures to visitors and schoolchildren and went to scientific meetings. On a dive in a freshwater sinkhole, she worked with a group that discovered human bones over seven thousand years old!

In 1959, Genie and her family moved to Siesta Key to be closer to Ilias's medical practice. Soon after the move, Genie's mother, Yumiko, died suddenly. Her death was a terrible shock to the whole family. Years later, Genie described her feelings. "I lost much interest in my work, felt I could no longer handle a full-time job, and thought I should stay home with the children and help my stepfather," she wrote.

At the Vanderbilts' suggestion, Genie closed the lab for a short time. Fortunately, she and Nobusan had some excellent help as they tried to recover from their grief and shock. Their new housekeeper, Geri Hinton, devoted herself to the family, especially young Niki. Within about six months, Genie went back to work and began the process of moving the lab to Siesta Key.

Although nothing was the same without Yumiko, life on Siesta Key was good. Genie was thrilled to see her children become expert swimmers and lovers of the sea. Even Niki, the youngest, could swim long distances underwater at the age of four. Hera was so used to seeing sharks at the lab that she hardly noticed when a five-foot-long shark swam past her on a diving trip. She was too busy watching a species of triggerfish that she had never seen before to pay attention to a shark!

Soon a new adventure awaited the children—a trip to the Red Sea. In 1964, Genie took the kids along on her investigation of a colony of over a thousand garden eels that lived in the waters near Elat, Israel. For Genie, this was the first of many research projects supported by the National Geographic Society. Garden eels are graceful, elusive creatures that make their homes on the sandy sea floor. They had never been caught in Elat. As the children waited at the water's surface, watching the action through their face masks, Genie approached the garden eel colony. As soon as she got close, the eels slithered into their burrows. Genie squirted formalin into the burrows, hoping it would lure the eels out. But none appeared. Just as Genie turned to swim away, she heard Hera splashing and yelling at the surface. An eel had come out! Quickly Genie grabbed the snaky creature. Back on the beach, a crowd gathered to see the first garden eel ever captured at Elat.

GARDEN EELS

The next day was just as exciting. Genie collected an odd-looking sand diver, a fish that burrows into the sand to hide. This small fish had a feathery dorsal fin, and Genie didn't think she had ever seen the species before. When she came out of the water, she put the fish in Niki's face mask until they could get a bucket. The strange sand diver turned out to be a previously unknown species of *Trichonotus*, which means "hairy back." Because Genie was the first scientist to describe it, she got to name it. She chose the name *Trichonotus nikii*, after her littlest helper.

Genie soon had the chance to share her discoveries with another young person who was interested in fish, the crown prince of Japan. At an early age, Prince Akihito had published reports on his studies of gobies. In the fall of 1965, Genie visited Japan and brought the prince an unusual gift—a small, trained nurse shark. (A saltwater tank was set up at the palace to receive it.) The nurse shark impressed everyone when it pushed a target for its food. The prince seemed pleased to meet Dr. Eugenie Clark, and she was greatly honored to meet the royalty of her mother's homeland.

BUTTERFLY FISH

Chapter 5
Shark Lady

At age forty-three, Eugenie Clark was named one of the top fourteen outstanding women in the United States by *Who's Who of American Women*. This was a tremendous honor, but she was too distracted by personal problems to be happy about the award. Ilias was caught up in both his medical practice and his business interests. He and Genie had grown apart. In 1967, Genie divorced Ilias and married a writer named Chandler Brossard.

Genie also made the difficult decision to leave the Cape Haze Marine Laboratory. She moved with her children back to New York, where she began teaching. Before Genie left Florida, she made sure the lab was in good hands. Perry Gilbert, a shark expert and friend of Genie's, became the new director. William Mote, a businessman who wanted to support marine research, also got involved with the lab's work. The lab was later renamed Mote Marine Laboratory, and it continued to support research and public education.

For the next few years, Genie was busier than ever. She kept working with the Mote Marine Laboratory as an advisor and trustee. She was also a visiting professor at the New England Institute for Medical Research for two years before joining the department of zoology at the University of Maryland. In 1969, she published her second book, *The Lady and the Sharks*. This book, which told the story of her years at the lab, reinforced her nickname, "Shark Lady."

Genie found that it wasn't easy for her to be a mother, writer, teacher, researcher, and wife. Her marriage to Chandler Brossard ended quickly. In 1970, she married Igor Klatzo, a scientist at the National Institute of Health, but this marriage didn't last either.

By 1973, at the age of fifty-one, Genie had settled into her teaching and research career at the University of Maryland. She was a popular professor because of her enthusiasm for her subject, and because of the slide shows and films she showed of her underwater adventures. From her comfortable house in a tree-lined neighborhood in Bethesda, Genie ventured off to do research in the Red Sea, Mexico, and Japan.

Genie works in her office at the University of Maryland.

It was in the Red Sea in 1973 that Genie studied another unusual fish. The Moses sole could release a poison that had an amazing effect on sharks, as Genie's lab tests showed. "We watched in disbelief as the big shark swam toward the tethered [Moses sole], opened wide its saw-toothed mouth, half enveloped the prey, and then— instant retreat," Genie wrote.

In addition to its effects on sharks, the sole's milky poison killed even the hardiest of small fish. After testing how much of the poison rats could tolerate, Genie, her assistants, and even fourteen-year-old Niki did a human taste test. The liquid tasted nasty and made their tongues pucker for twenty minutes. No wonder the lab's sharks dodged the Moses sole instead of munching it! To confirm how fish in the wild would react to the sole, Genie and her helpers set out a line in the Red Sea. The line was baited with Moses soles and a variety of other fish. By the next morning, all the fish had been eaten—except the soles.

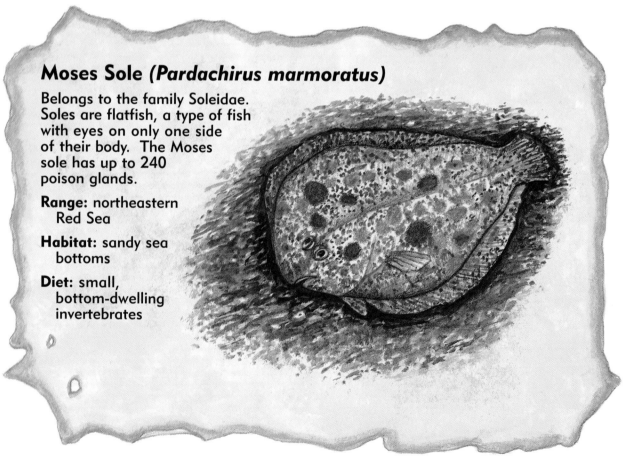

Moses Sole (*Pardachirus marmoratus*)

Belongs to the family Soleidae. Soles are flatfish, a type of fish with eyes on only one side of their body. The Moses sole has up to 240 poison glands.

Range: northeastern Red Sea

Habitat: sandy sea bottoms

Diet: small, bottom-dwelling invertebrates

In April of 1975, Genie appeared on the cover of *National Geographic* magazine, posing next to what looked like a sleeping shark in an underwater cave near Isla Mujeres, Mexico. Though she had already written several articles for this popular magazine, the sleeping shark story may have been the most dramatic. How could a diver safely pose next to a fierce creature like a shark? And since scientists believed that sharks needed to swim constantly to keep water flowing over their gills, how could sharks sleep?

Genie had first learned about sleeping sharks years earlier, when a Mexican naturalist named Ramon Bravo told her how the sharks that came to the underwater caves near Isla Mujeres seemed to go into a trance. Later, Genie visited to investigate the mystery. With the help of other scientists, Mexican divers, and her daughter Aya, Genie studied the conditions of the underwater caves. The researchers learned that the sharks weren't really sleeping, and that they could breathe by pumping water over their gills as they lay in the caves. They also found that the cave water had less salt and more oxygen than regular ocean water. Was the oxygen-rich water causing the sharks to "sleep"?

Genie and her helpers also made some interesting observations about remoras, small fish that hitch rides on sharks by anchoring themselves with a sucker. Remoras use their teeth to remove parasites—tiny, crablike creatures that live on or in other animals—from a shark's skin. The scientists observed a remora cleaning a "sleeping" shark's entire body with ease in one of the underwater caves.

Genie and her colleagues knew that the less salt a body of water has, the more easily parasites come off a fish in that water. They also knew that many biologists believed certain fish enter freshwater to get rid of parasites. Were the sharks doing the same thing? Although she didn't find definite answers to the sleeping shark puzzle, Genie and her readers were fascinated by the experience.

LEMON SHARK WITH
REMORAS

Over the next few years, Genie continued to investigate garden eels, "sleeping" sharks, and poisonous soles. The more she wrote about sharks, the more she became known as the Shark Lady, even though she studied many other fish. When her film *The Sharks* was shown in 1982, it attracted more viewers than any other public television program to that date. Genie became more of a public figure than ever.

As she traveled and dived throughout the world, Genie grew disturbed by what she saw happening to coral reefs. More and more, people were developing seaside resorts, drilling into the seafloor for oil, and dumping garbage in the ocean. These activities were destroying underwater habitats, leaving fish without homes and food. Genie started to write articles to educate people about the importance of protecting the marine environment.

One area that particularly concerned Genie was the rich reefs of Ras Muhammad, Egypt, where she had been diving for years. While diving there, she became friends with an enthusiastic young diver who happened to be the son of Egypt's president, Anwar Sadat. Genie was later able to meet with President Sadat and to convince him of the need to protect the area. In 1983, Ras Muhammad became Egypt's first national park.

Guard the Sea

Protection for fish is needed more than ever. Many fish live and breed in waters that are threatened by pollution, and the activities that made Genie worry about coral reefs still take place in our tropical seas. You can help protect fish, whether they live in a faraway place like the Red Sea or a local stream. Here's how to find out what you can do:

✔ Visit the Center for Marine Conservation, an organization dedicated to protecting water-dwelling creatures and their habitats, at www.cmc-ocean.org

✔ Visit Reef Relief, an organization dedicated to protecting coral reefs, at www.reefrelief.org

✔ Contact the local fish and game or natural resources department and ask about ways to help fish in your state.

Over fifty years had passed since Genie had first read about William Beebe's deep dives in the Bahamas and dreamed of diving herself. In 1987, at an age when many people retire, sixty-five-year-old Genie started a new adventure. She began to dive in submersibles—small underwater crafts that look a little like submarines. Plunging as far as twelve thousand feet into the ocean, Genie and her colleagues observed the huge animals of the deep, including sharks as long as a motor home. Since she began diving in submersibles, Genie has explored deep waters all over the world, making a total of more than seventy dives.

Imagine having a grandmother who is a famous underwater explorer. In 1990, Aya gave birth to her son, Eli—Genie's first grandchild. When Eli was a year old, Genie published her first children's book, *The Desert Beneath the Sea*, with author Ann McGovern. The book tells the stories of many unusual animals that live on the sandy seafloor.

Genie and her grandson, Eli

The same year, Genie traveled to Ningaloo Reef Marine Park in Western Australia to study the world's biggest fish, the whale shark. She felt entirely safe diving among the gentle giants, which feed only on tiny creatures. Her encounters reminded her of an adventure she had had years before, when she took a ride on a passing whale shark. "I was crazy," Genie told an interviewer. "We wanted to study and photograph her. She was well over forty feet long. Once I got on her, I couldn't let go. And I went far away from the photographers and the boat. The shark was cruising along steadily at three knots, and, after a while, I thought to myself, Why am I still holding onto the shark, getting farther away from the boat? And I finally let go."

In a *National Geographic* article on whale sharks, Genie wrote about how this kind of play could be harmful if too many people engaged in it. This was happening in Ningaloo Reef Marine Park. Genie had inspired many of her readers to become divers, just as William Beebe had inspired her. She realized that she also had to inspire them to become protectors of marine life.

Though Genie retired from full-time teaching in 1992, she continues to teach occasionally at the University of Maryland. She also conducts research in the Caribbean, the Red Sea, the Solomon Islands, Papua New Guinea, and Palau, where she collected fish so many years ago. "I plan to keep diving and researching and conserving until I'm ninety years old," Genie once said. She doesn't show signs of slowing down in any part of her life. In 1997, she married an old friend, Henry Yoshinobu Kon. And in 1999, at the age of seventy-six, she went diving in Papua New Guinea with her old friend from school, Norma. Spending part of each year in Sarasota, Florida, Genie continues her association with scientists at the Mote Marine Laboratory and throughout the world.

As you gaze into a fish tank, a lake, or the shifting waters of the sea, picture yourself as an underwater explorer. Can you see yourself following watery trails and unraveling fishy questions? Can you imagine yourself spending your days learning about fish and working to protect them? Like Eugenie Clark, you may have a lifetime of wet and wonderful adventures awaiting you.

Genie and Henry at their wedding in 1997

Important Dates

1922—Eugenie Clark is born on May 4 in New York City.

1942—Receives degree from Hunter College

1946—Receives master's degree from New York University. Studies at Scripps Institution of Oceanography

1949—Travels to South Pacific islands to study and collect fish

1950—Receives Ph.D. from New York University and Fulbright scholarship to study fish in the Red Sea. Marries Ilias Papakonstantinou

1952—Daughter Hera born

1953—Publishes *Lady with a Spear*

1954—Daughter Aya born

1955—Moves to Florida to become director of Cape Haze Marine Laboratory

1956—Son Tak born

1958—Son Nikolas born

1959—Mother dies

1967—Divorces Ilias Papakonstantinou. Moves to New York

1969—Begins teaching at University of Maryland. Publishes *The Lady and the Sharks*

1972—Studies garden eels near Elat, Israel

1975—Studies "sleeping" sharks in Mexico

1983—Helps establish Egypt's first national park

1987—Makes her first dive in a submersible

1992—Retires from full-time teaching. Awarded honorary doctorate from University of Massachusetts

1995—Awarded honorary doctorates from University of Guelph and Long Island University

1997—Marries Henry Yoshinobu Kon

Glossary

anatomy: the study of the structure of living things

biology: the study of living things

crustacean: an animal with a hard outer skeleton and two pairs of antennae. Lobsters and shrimps are crustaceans.

estuary: the area where a river runs into the sea, mixing freshwater and salt water

hermaphrodite: an animal with both male and female organs

hybrid: an animal or plant that is produced by parents of different species, varieties, or breeds

ichthyologist: a scientist who studies fish

invertebrate: an animal with no backbone

naturalist: a person who studies nature

species: a group of plants or animals with common traits, especially the means of creating young

vertebrate: an animal with a backbone

zoology: the study of animals

Bibliography

Balon, Eugene K. "The Life and Work of Eugenie Clark: Devoted to Diving and Science." *Environmental Biology of Fishes* 41 (1994): 89–114.

Clark, Eugenie, and Ann McGovern. *The Desert Beneath the Sea.* New York: Scholastic, 1991.

Clark, Eugenie, John F. Pohle, and David C. Shen. "Ecology and Population Dynamics of Garden Eels at Ras Mohammed, Red Sea." *National Geographic Research and Exploration* 6 (1990): 306-318.

Clark, Eugenie. "Flashlight Fish of the Red Sea." *National Geographic,* November 1978, 719–728.

Clark, Eugenie. "Into the Lairs of 'Sleeping' Sharks." *National Geographic,* April 1975, 570–584.

Clark, Eugenie. *The Lady and the Sharks.* New York: Harper and Row, 1969.

Clark, Eugenie. *Lady with a Spear.* New York: Harper, 1953.

Clark, Eugenie. "Mating of Groupers." *Natural History* 74 (1965): 22–25.

Clark, Eugenie. "Sharks at 2,000 Feet." *National Geographic,* November 1986, 681–691.

Clark, Eugenie. "Whale Sharks: Gentle Monsters of the Deep." *National Geographic,* December 1992, 123–138.

*Coleman, Lori. *My Pet Fish.* Minneapolis: Lerner Publications, 1998.

*Cone, Molly. *Come Back, Salmon.* San Francisco: Sierra Club Books, 1994.

LaBastille, Anne. *Women and Wilderness.* San Francisco: Sierra Club Books, 1980.

*MacQuitty, Miranda. *Shark.* New York: Knopf, 1992.

*McGovern, Ann. *Shark Lady: True Adventures of Eugenie Clark.* New York: Scholastic, 1978.

*Mills, Dick, and Gwynne Vevers. *The Golden Encyclopedia of Freshwater Tropical Aquarium Fishes.* New York: Golden Books, 1982.

Moyle, Peter B. *Fish: An Enthusiast's Guide.* Berkeley, Calif.: University of California Press, 1993.

*Zim, Herbert S., and Hurst H. Shoemaker. *Fishes.* New York: Golden Books, 1987.

*An asterisk indicates a book for young readers.

All quotations in this book were taken from the above sources.

All photographs in this book are reproduced courtesy of Eugenie Clark, except: © Andreas Rechnitzer, front cover; © Ruth Petzold, p. 4; © Bev Rodgerson, p. 39.

Index